{familia}

A CHAPBOOK BY K. M. CLAUDE

COPYRIGHT © 2016 K. M. CLAUDE

PUBLISHED BY nonSENSE PRESS

HTTP://NONSENSEPRESS.COM/
ISBN-13: 978-0692632253 † ISBN-10: 0692632255

earlier versions of these poems first
appeared in chapbook form with layout and
design by Anneliese DePano for a poetry course.

{ TABLE OF CONTENTS }

{familia}

familia cæsar (*romæ antiquæ*)

CALIGULA ... *sidus* | madman | god-brother | emperor
DRUSILLA ... *cara* | green-eyed | sister-wife | lover

familia tiefer (*louisianæ*)

ANNEMARIE ... *whore* | drunk | serpent-tongue | cunt-bearing caligula
EMILEIN ... *fag* | monster | pretty-boy | unwilling drusilla

Two timelines:

> points come unplotted, paths diverge;
> stories get told, retold, untold.

New names:

> star becomes *meretrix*;
> beloved, *impudicus*.

Swapped surnames, found faces:

> god-brother emperor bears fairer features;
> sister-wife lover grows pretty-boy penis.

Fact is fiction and fiction a history:

> nothing truly changes;
> one family, overall.

Blessed babe in baby boots;
ruddy   reddened   *caligæ*
on   ruby-crowned   Caligula,
my star   (my king.)

You   fill   those   shoes
red   shoes,   blood   shoes
blood   boots,   blood   red
(too red)   so well.

Grow   into   your   boots
blood   boots,   blood   shoes
silk   shoes,   soft   sheets,
sidus   star-child.

Sweetest star, the cent'ries change:
your face is fair, your sex is soft,
yet you've filled your boots
(blood boots)   *too* well.

LOVE

she shoves him on sheets, palms spit-slicked, slips
fingers against him, inside him, right through him—
his   heart,   his   soul,   his   self   in   herself—
      so it's

           love

makes her slide up, spread-legged, situated astride
(not   side-saddle)   and   sit,   swap   spit,   slip
dick   inside   pussy-cunt   dripping   in   pussy-cum.
      she calls it

           "love"

while he writhes underneath her and whimpers—
wishing   she   wouldn't,   wanting   she   couldn't,
('cause cunt burns like fire to fag baby-brother)
coming   undone   anyway — and   thinks   that   it's
          love.

brother lay beside me
at the banquet to
celebrate his godhood.
like siblings,
            we kissed
and carried on
through the changing
of courses, custom
dictating that i must
exchange seats with
our sisters
            but
brother lay beside me,
did not let me move.
brother sipped wine,
said nothing, fed
me on dormice 'til
like man and wife
            we kissed.
the guests all said
nothing while god-
brother lay beside me,
enjoying his supper,
picking which sister
he loved most of all.
            later, much later,
            once everyone left,
brother lay inside me
his sister-wife empress.

MADMAN'S MONSTER, WHORE'S LOVER

"brother, lay beside me,"
spills spit-slicked through split-lips
from sordid sister, salacious sister, incestuous sister's
serpent mouth hissing obscenities, spitting sex
like a sacred incantation sprinkled with
sighs and moans and insubstantial promises
that drown out his sobs

         (she has a thousand lovers
         yet it's precious fag brother-
         cum-husband
         she loves most of all.)

NAMES
AND
TIMES
CHANGE

{ELDER
SISTER
RAPE
BROTHER}

{KING-
SON
CONQUER
SISTER}

BUT
MONSTERS
ARE
ETERNAL.

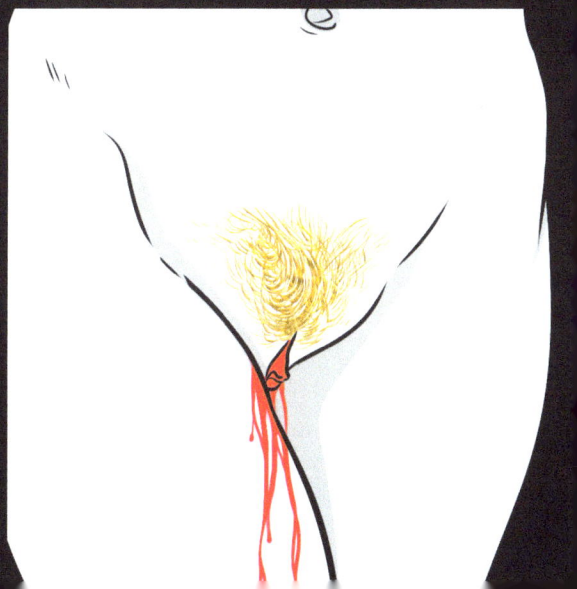

DRUSILLA'S ROUND (THE RISE AND FALL)

(in the whore's kitchen)

i thought about killing you yesterday
but i hadn't had my coffee yet.
lucky bitch.

i gave you cock three nights ago
for dinner. you forced milk down
my throat (again)

i don't care for country matters
yet you force me to dine on nothing.
fuck off.

you stink of fish and raw meat
don't tell me it'll taste like roses.
please don't

no more.

(by the madman's bed)

he slid a finger deep inside her.
cunt. i wish he'd rip her
inside out.

fuck me
the way you do those boys, those girls:
a piece of meat, bloody-red, bleeding-raw.

ride me
the way you ride your horse:
make it a parade, make it a spectacle

please me
like a servant or a slave before your siblings
let them see who your favorite is

Open little pretty-boy,
open open wide.
Your sister wants to play
and all her beaus are gone.

{unwilling drusilla,
your empress calls}

Open little pretty-boy,
always open for a ride.
Just a kiss, she says and strips
and asks you to play along.

{sister-whore's fag-brother,
don't look so appalled}

Open little pretty-boy,
give away your pride.
A kiss from head to head. She lied
and said "This won't take long."

{come for caligula,
give her your all}

Close up little pretty-boy,
pretend to be just fine
Your sister really needed you.
Pretend like nothing's wrong.

whore sits on fag's face, straddles sternum,
bleeds black-blood vag-blood into mouth,
'til fag drowns in cunt-water, dark-water, rag-water

whore rides 'til he drowns, lets him come
up for air, spit black-blood, snake-blood
'til she tugs at his hair, pushes down, pushes in with

> (whore tongue, snake tongue, her tongue against
> tongue, tasting self, tasting hell, tasting cunt—
>
> bearing god-brother madman whose tongue
> is her tongue, whose self she's become above
>
> unwilling drusilla, her brother, her lover whom
> she rides like a stallion, paraded hailed king
>
> hail sister, hail *sidus*, hail cunt-bearing caligula
> hail torturer, hail emperor, hail jupiter, *hail*)

whore slips away, pussy-slicked, fag silent and
spitting up blood of the cunt-christ god up above
'til she kisses him hard, supreme power secured.

Plump, pouty lips
(once pink peaches from lively lipstick,
now hued, blued; perfect purple plums)
stay supple and
downturned —
crescent blood oranges drip juices down
past pomegranate dimpled cheeks,
            now chalky
            like a mulberry
            pre-Pyramus and Thisbe
into sticky matted hair, knotted by wetness
both whites and reds.

{Beloved sister!
            Behold your monstrous brother,
            former lover to your Caligulean lust,
            your damned drunken divinity
                        —was it worth the cost?}

I spread lifeless roots
(twisted limbs, rigid muscles, lifeless legs)
            and from purpling lips
            (once peach pink)
                  I drink
                  to your health
                        no more.}

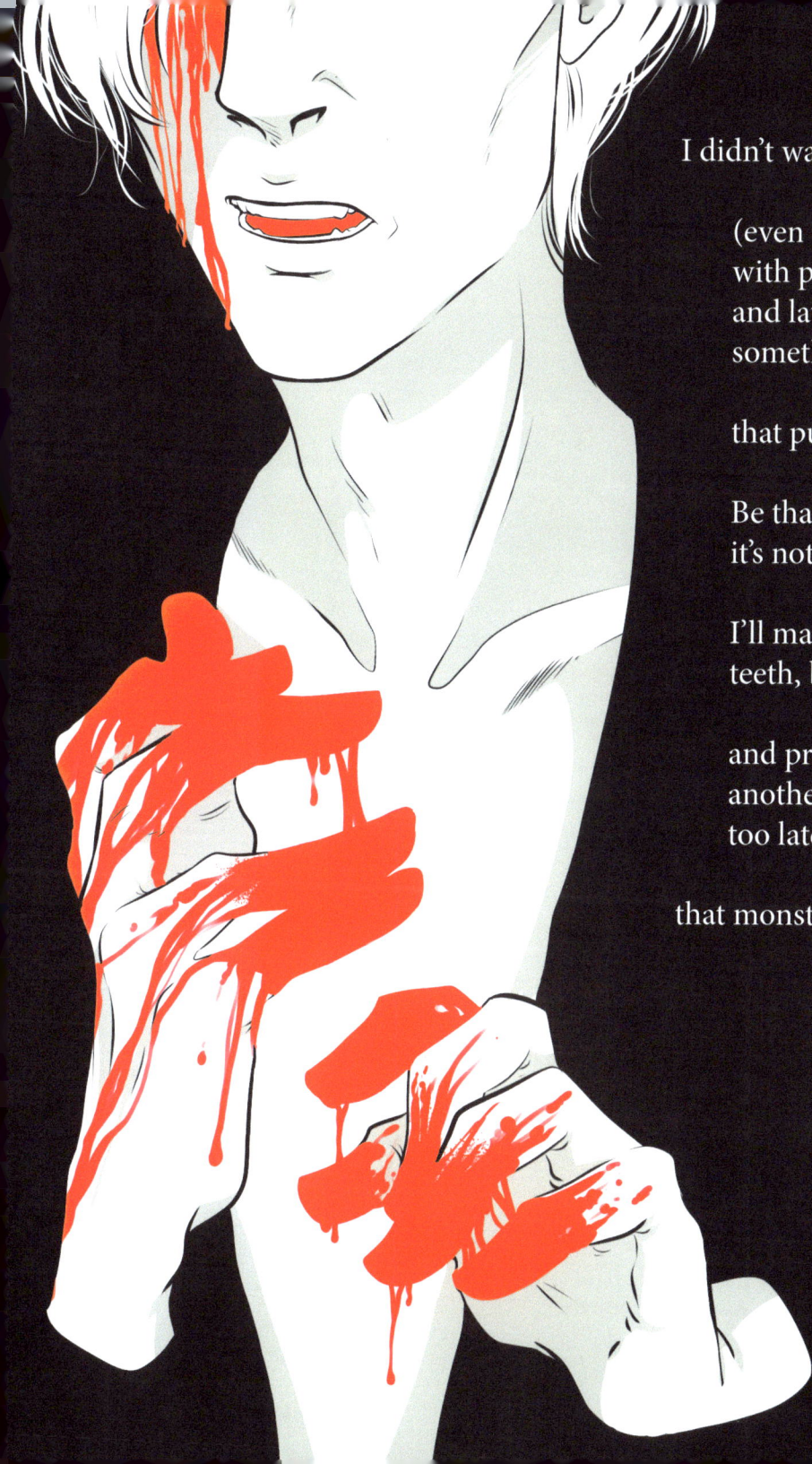

I didn't want to believe

(even as I push past pink flesh
with pink sticky fingers
and later plunge in with
something much pinker
        much redder, much thicker
that pulses and punctures —
        Quit crying!
Be thankful
it's not the knife this time,
        not yet.
I'll make a necklace of your teen-boy
teeth, barrettes of your finger-bones
        pretty gifts
and pretty toys from and for
another little pretty-boy
too late to realize)

that monstrosity was contagious…

…AND I AM ILL.

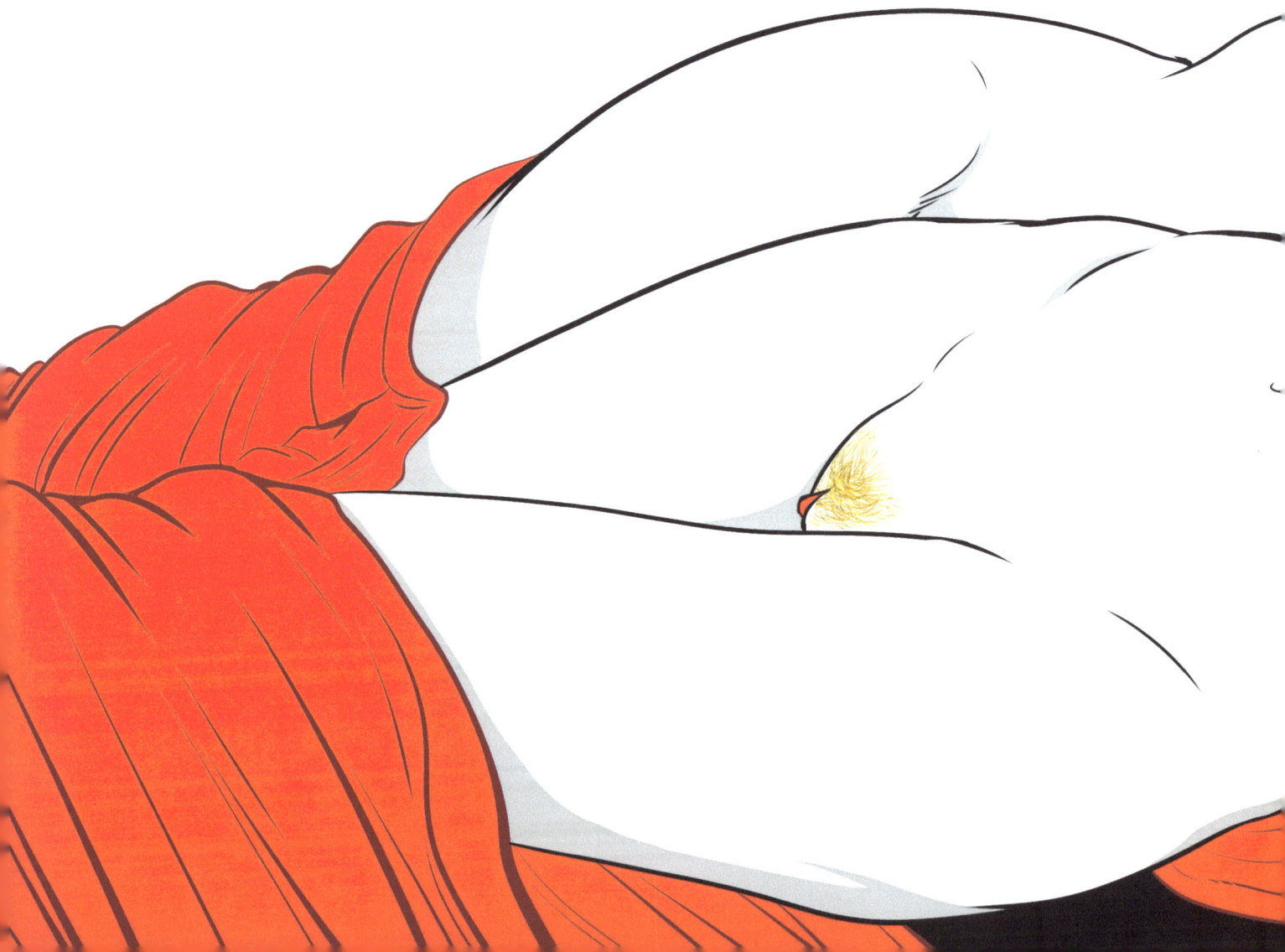

{SIDUS ET CARA}

{FAGGOT AND WHORE}

"...amo te..."

{ NOTES }

DRAMATIS PERSONÆ
> *sidus* — star
> *cara* — beloved, precious, or expensive

THIS IS A TALE WITH TOO MUCH TRUTH TO IT
> *meretrix* — harlot, whore
> *impundicus* — shameless, licentious, homosexual

THE FAMILY AFFAIR
> Roman custom dictated that the male and female heads of house —
> that is, the husband and wife — hold the seats of honor at dinner; in
> the case of a Roman bachelor, his sisters were to share the hostess' seat
> of honor without exclusivity.

ἀνάγκη
> ἀνάγκη (anánkē) is necessity beyond supplication, dictator of all fates
> of every time and place, to which even the divine is bound (so what
> hope has man?)

SIDUS ET CARA {FAGGOT AND WHORE}
> *amo te* — {a lie}

{ACKNOWLEDGEMENTS}

GRATIAS ANNELIESÆ AGO: without you this would be only words words words

{ about the author }
K. M. CLAUDE IS AN ONLY CHILD

www.ingramcontent.com/pod-product-compliance
Lightning Source LLC
Chambersburg PA
CBHW042115040426
42448CB00003B/288